Investigate

Senses

Sue Barraclough

Heinemann
LIBRARY

www.heinemann.co.uk/library
Visit our website to find out more information about Heinemann Library books.

To order:
☎ Phone 44 (0) 1865 888066

🖹 Send a fax to 44 (0) 1865 314091

💻 Visit the Heinemann Bookshop at www.heinemann.co.uk/library to browse our catalogue and order online.

Heinemann Library is an imprint of Pearson Education Limited, a company incorporated in England and Wales having its registered office at Edinburgh Gate, Harlow, Essex, CM20 2JE – Registered company number: 00872828

Heinemann is a registered trademark of Pearson Education Ltd.
Text © Pearson Education Limited 2008
First published in hardback in 2008
Paperback edition first published in 2009

Edited by Sarah Shannon, Catherine Clarke, and Laura Knowles
Designed by Joanna Hinton-Malivoire, Victoria Bevan, and Hart McLeod
Picture research by Liz Alexander
Production by Duncan Gilbert
Originated by Chroma Graphics (Overseas) Pte. Ltd
Printed and bound in China by Leo Paper Group

ISBN 978 0 431932 83 5 (hardback)
12 11 10 09 08
10 9 8 7 6 5 4 3 2 1

ISBN 978 0 431933 02 3 (paperback)
13 12 11 10 09
10 9 8 7 6 5 4 3 2 1

British Library Cataloguing in Publication Data
Barraclough, Sue
  Senses. - (Investigate)
  573.8'7
BA full catalogue record for this book is available from the British Library.

Acknowledgements
We would like to thank the following for permission to reproduce photographs: ©Alamy pp. **9** (UpperCut Images), **12** (ImageState), **15** (Geoff du Feu), **16** (Westend61), **17** (Adams Picture Library t/a apl), **25** (Juniors Bildarchiv), **26** (marc Hill), **28** (JUPITERIMAGES/BananaStock), **29** (Peter Griffin); ©Corbis pp. **7** (Auslöser/zefa), **14** (Paul Souders), **19** (David Brabyn), **24** (Chad Weckler); ©Creatas p. **8** (Thinkstock); ©Getty Images pp. **10** (altrendo images), **22** (Frank Rothe/Taxi); ©Pearson Education Ltd. p. **4** (Malcom Harris. 2005); ©Photolibrary pp. **5** (Stockbyte), **21** (BSIP Medical); ©PunchStock p. **20** (Digital Vision).

Cover photograph of hand touching crop reproduced with permission of ©Alamy (Blackout Concepts).

Every effort has been made to contact copyright holders of material reproduced in this book. Any omissions will be rectified in subsequent printings if notice is given to the publishers.

Contents

Some words are shown in bold, **like this**. You can find out what they mean by looking in the glossary.

The sensory system

Your body has five main senses. Your senses help you to:

⟶ see
⟶ hear
⟶ smell
⟶ taste
⟶ touch and feel.

Your senses tell you what is happening in the world around you. Your five senses make up your **sensory system**.

Your senses help you to understand sounds, colours, shapes, and smells. Your senses can warn you of dangers. For example, your sense of touch warns you if something is hot so that you will not be hurt.

 Your senses of smell and taste let you know if food is not safe to eat.

Your brain **controls** your senses. Your brain works with your senses to help you understand what is happening around you.

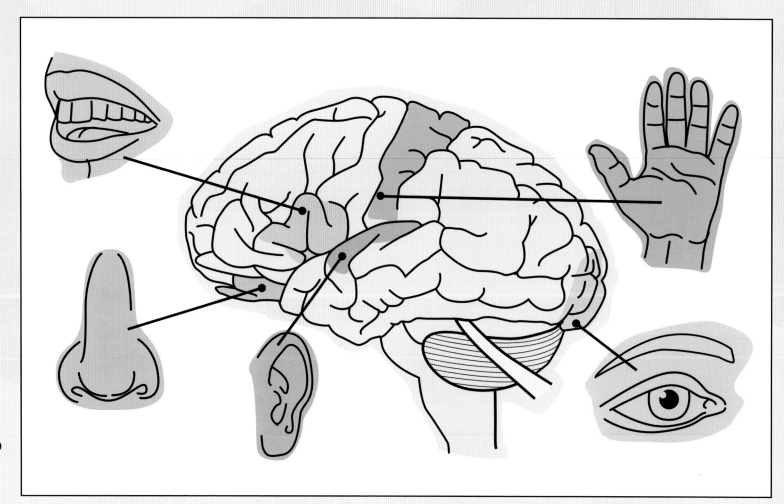

Your body has different parts such as your eyes and ears. These parts collect information about how things look or sound. This information is sent to your brain.

Seeing

Your sense of sight helps you to see colours and shapes. It also helps you see moving objects and tell how far away they are.

CLUE

- What happens when you close your eyes?

9

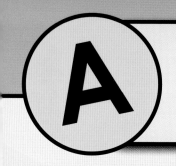

A Your eyes and your brain.

Light bounces off objects into your eye. Light goes through an opening in your eye called the **pupil**. Your eye makes a picture of what you are looking at.

The picture is sent along a **nerve** to your brain.
Your brain helps you understand what you see.

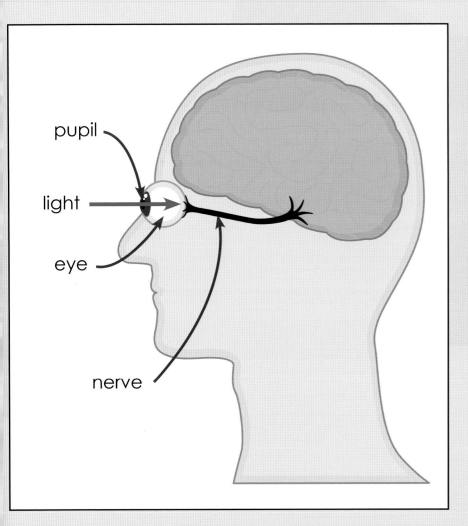

pupil

light

eye

nerve

ANIMAL EYE FACTS

➠ Eagles fly through the sky looking for small animals to catch. They have very good eyesight.

➠ Moles live in the dark under the ground. They have very poor eyesight.

Hearing

Your ears help you to hear sounds all around you. The outer part of the ear is shaped to pick up sounds.

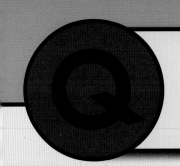
Your ears can pick up soft and loud sounds. The sounds are taken into a tunnel called the **ear canal**. The sounds travel into your ear and **signals** are sent to the brain.

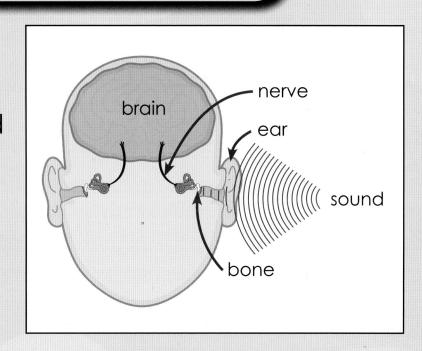

brain

nerve

ear

sound

bone

CLUES

- Do fish have ears?

- Where are a bird's ears?

13

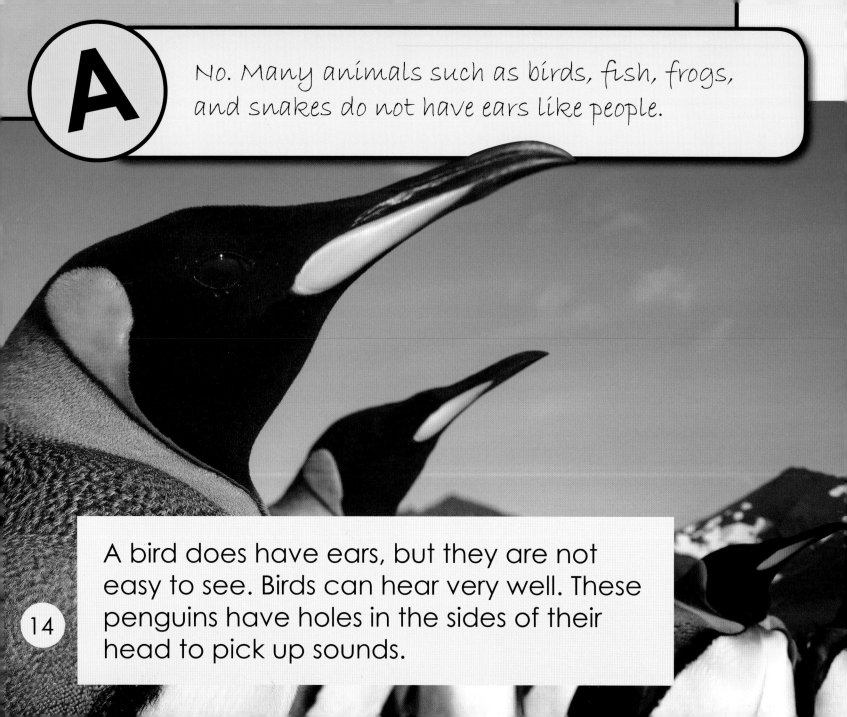

A No. Many animals such as birds, fish, frogs, and snakes do not have ears like people.

A bird does have ears, but they are not easy to see. Birds can hear very well. These penguins have holes in the sides of their head to pick up sounds.

Some animals have very big ears. They need to have good hearing to make sure they can hear what is happening around them. Their ears are shaped to pick up the smallest sounds.

Hares need to listen out for **predators**. Their big ears help them to pick up small sounds.

Smelling

Your nose helps you smell things. Smells are in the air around you. Your sense of smell is useful and it can keep you safe. Your nose tells you if food smells **rotten**. The smell of smoke warns you of danger from fire.

Why do you have hairs in your nose?

? **CLUES**

- Does air usually go through your nose or your mouth when you breathe in?

- Why do you think you sneeze?

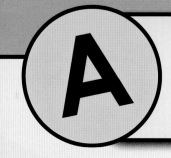

A Hairs in your nose catch dust and dirt in the air as you breathe in.

signals are sent to your brain along a **nerve**

your brain tells you what the smell is

tiny parts in your nose sense the smell

nose

air goes into your nose

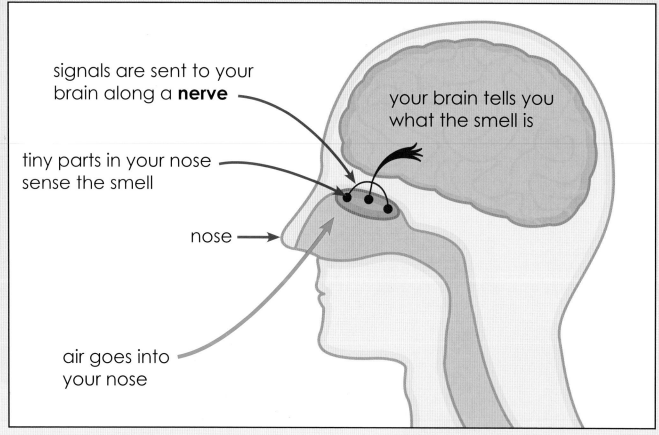

 This diagram shows how you recognise smells.

Dogs have a very good sense of smell. The police use dogs to help them find things or people.

19

Tasting

Your sense of taste tells you about things you eat. It tells you if something tastes good or bad. Foods have different tastes. Apples taste sweet. Lemons taste sour.

 Which body parts help you to taste?

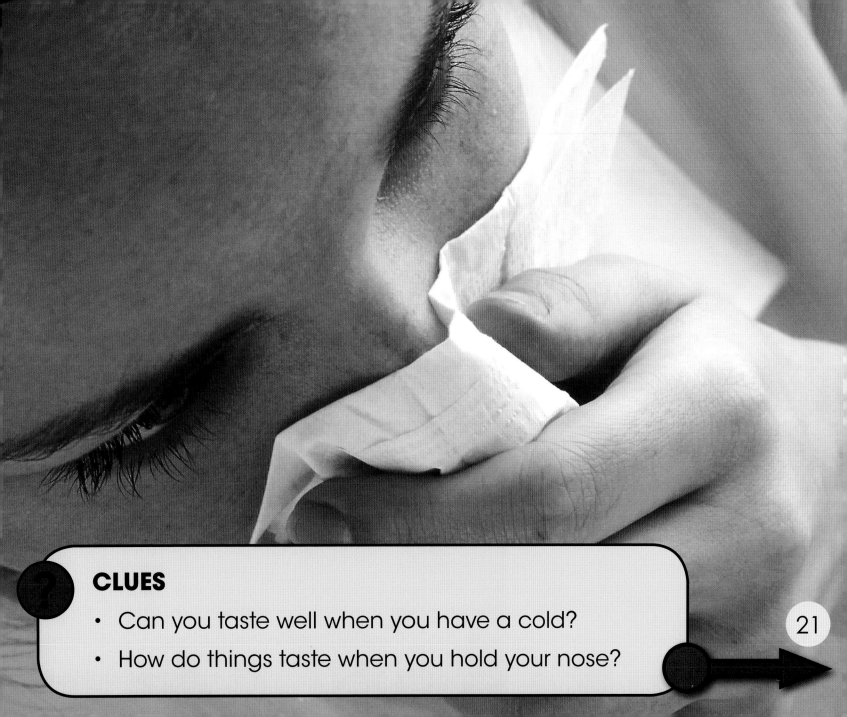

CLUES

- Can you taste well when you have a cold?
- How do things taste when you hold your nose?

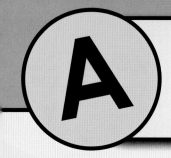 You use your tongue, your nose, and your brain to taste things.

Your tongue is covered in tiny taste buds. Taste buds pick up different tastes such as sweet or salty.

Your taste buds send information to your brain. As your tongue tastes something, smells float up into your nose. Your tongue and your nose send information to your brain.

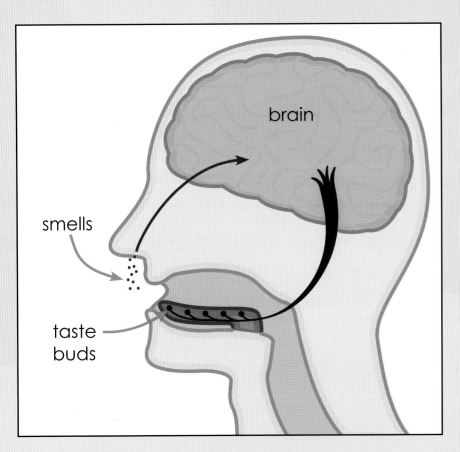

brain

smells

taste buds

ANIMAL TASTE FACTS

➠ Flies taste things with their feet.

➠ A snake uses its tongue to taste and smell.

⬅ This diagram shows how you recognise tastes.

23

Touching and feeling

Your sense of touch tells you how things feel.
Things can feel soft or hard, rough or smooth.
Things can feel hot or cold, wet or dry.

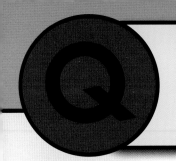

Q Which parts of your body do you use most to feel things?

CLUE

- What do you use to stroke a cat's soft fur?

25

A Your fingers.

You have tiny parts called **nerve endings** under your skin. Each one senses something different. It sends messages to your brain about how things feel.

Every part of your body has long, thin parts called **nerves** that connect the nerve endings to your brain. Nerves carry information in the same way as the wires in a telephone carry a voice.

This diagram shows how the nerves in your body are connected to your brain. →

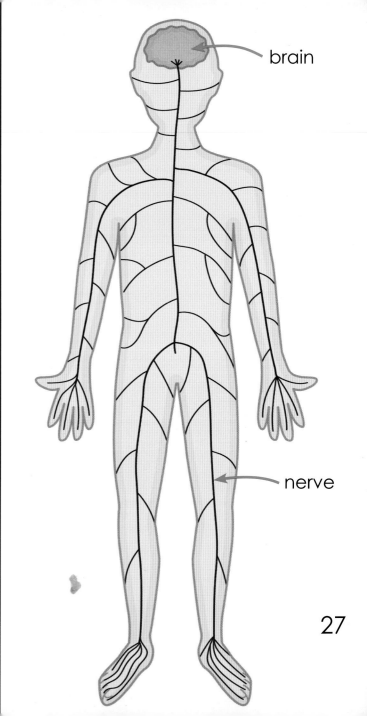

brain

nerve

27

Making sense of the world

Your senses work with your brain to help you to understand and learn about the world around you. Your brain stores lots of information about how things look, sound, feel, taste, and smell. Your senses play a part in everything you do.

The world is full of noises, smells, tastes, feelings, colours, and shapes. Your **sensory system** sends information to your brain so that you know what to do and how to move.

Checklist

Your senses can help you to:
- see
- hear
- smell
- taste
- touch and feel.

Your brain **controls** your **sensory system**.

Glossary

control make something work

ear canal tunnel inside your ear that sounds travel down

nerve long, thin fibre that carries messages between your brain and other parts of your body

nerve ending tiny shaped part at the end of a nerve. It picks up information about how things feel.

predator animal that feeds on other animals

pupil the round, black hole at the front of your eye that lets in light

rotten food that has gone bad and is not safe to eat

sensory system all the parts of your body that work together to help you see, hear, taste, smell and feel

signals messages that are carried along nerves to your brain

Index